RICKY MARTIN

backstage pass

YOUR LA VIDA LOCA KEEPSAKE SCRAPBOOK

BY KIMBERLY WALSH

SCHOLASTIC INC.
New York Toronto London Auckland Sydney
Mexico City New Delhi Hong Kong

ISBN 0-439-15329-8

Guide To What's Inside

Introduction

"La Vida Loca, that's my life right now. I am going through an adrenaline rush that my career is giving me . . . and it's pretty intense."

—Ricky Martin, to a New York City newspaper

¡QUÉ CALIENTE!

Think Ricky Martin is lava-hot now? Check it: The day he was born, an entire nation turned out in festive finery and celebrated big time! *True.* But not because the whole country instantly recognized a brand-new shining star in its midst. It just so happens that the debut of tiny Enrique Martin Morales fell on December 24, "Noche Buena," the day Puerto Ricans traditionally reserve for their blowout Christmas jubilation. Families gather, feasts are served, and children get their presents.

So Ricky was born under a lucky star.

Coincidence? Or sign of things to come? Either way you slice it, Ricky Martin is *still* inspiring spontaneous bouts of combustive exhilaration everywhere he goes. And he goes, pretty much, to every corner of the earth.

RICKY MARTIN MANIA!

"The first global superstar," is how the media tags Ricky, and despite the hype, it just may be true. Pick a country, anywhere, on any continent — now check the record charts and the concert halls. Chances are Ricky rules, and with good reason. Music may be the universal language, but Ricky is one of the few singers who records multilingually. His albums are sung in Spanish, Portuguese, and French, and prior to 1999, he sold more than 15 million of 'em. His most recent Spanish-language album, *Vuelve,* went to Number One in 22 different countries.

When Ricky performed live on NBC's The Today Show in June, "fandemonium" erupted!

Oh, yeah — one more thing. He's now singing in English. And on the scale of global superstardom, that takes him over the top. Like another worldwide superstar once warbled, "If I can make it there, I'll make it anywhere," and the release of his first album in English, *Ricky Martin*, sealed it: He's now made it everywhere.

La Vida Loca

There have been *mucho* magic moments in Ricky's glittering career, but none quite so amazing as his performance at the 1999 Grammy Awards. That was the Ricky Martin Moment for the millennium. Forget even that he won the award for Best Latin Pop song. It was, of course, his electrifying performance of *"La Copa de la Vida"* (The Cup of Life) that ignited mass adulation — that had hearts pumping, audiences jumping, and superstars bumping into each other backstage just to get a word with him.

Ever since that moment, followed quickly by the release of the red-hot single, "Livin' *La Vida Loca*," and *Ricky Martin,* the album, Ricky has busted out. He's been on the cover of nearly every major American magazine, from *Time* to *Entertainment Weekly* to *Rolling Stone*. He's charmed TV talk show hosts Rosie O'Donnell and Jay Leno; he's scorched *Saturday Night Live* and *The Today Show* with his volcanic performances. He's hosted and performed on awards shows, too. Beyond the Grammys, fans have seen him on the World Music Awards and the MTV Awards.

What inspires Ricky's love songs? Pain and heartache are two major subjects — "That's when it becomes music."

THE REAL RICKY

So who *is* this explosive talent who's setting records, setting pulses racing, and jetting off as the superstar of the millennium? Funny you should ask. Over the next forty or so photo- and fact-filled pages, you're about to find out. Ricky's story is as exciting, uplifting, and inspiring as he is. Maybe it seems like all it took was a song, a smile, and a swivel, but that doesn't quite tell it all. As Ricky reminds people, "I want to be humble about it, but I have been doing this for a long time."

When Ricky is mobbed by fans, he admits it's kinda fun. "This is madness," he says. "It's just crazy, but I love it!"

Little Ricky

Song stylist, musician, composer, electric performer: In the world of music, this boy does it all — in several languages — and snarfs up awards like a runaway vacuum. Movie star, TV player, stage actor: In the world of drama, this boy *also* does it all — bilingually — and yep, has a mantel full of trophies for his efforts. You get the picture: Ricky Martin totally defines multitalented. Check it: ain't nothing new. He prepared for all of it. And he started young.

"When I was six years old, I said to my father, 'Daddy, I want to be an artist,' " Ricky recalls. "He was like, 'Really, how can I help you?' He found me my first audition for a commercial."

Even before he joined Menudo, an eight-year-old "Enrique" was performing at local shows and productions in his hometown of Santurce, Puerto Rico.

Ricky was born on December 24, 1971, in Santurce on the island nation of Puerto Rico. Called by his given name, Enrique, he was raised in its biggest city, San Juan. His dad Enrique was a psychologist; his mom, Nereida, an accountant and legal secretary. Little Ricky was their only child, and they divorced when he was two years old. The seeds of an unhappy childhood? Nuh-*uh*! Quite the opposite. In his official biography and in many interviews, Ricky has used practically the same exact words to describe his early life. "My childhood was very healthy, near to my parents who were divorced. I did whatever I wanted; I lived with my mother, if I wanted to be with her, and with my father in the same way. I had the same affection from both of them. Although they were no longer married, they were very good friends."

Raised in the Catholic religion, he was an altar boy for many years. "I had a real good time," he told *Interview* magazine. "I would ring the bell — that was the best part of it. Clang, clang, clang! The priest would look at me: 'Okay, enough is enough!' "

At home, the only child was never a lonely child. For Ricky grew up alongside his older half brothers: two boys from his mom's earlier marriage. They were a huge influence on his young life, especially in their choice of music.

"When I was a kid," he said in *USA Today*, "my brothers and I were all into rock, rock, rock. I think the first album I bought was a David Bowie album, and the second was from the band Journey. In those days, Latin bands were not hip for my generation. So I grew up listening to [groups like] Boston and Cheap Trick." In an on-line interview, he added, "[Until] one day, our mother got tired of rock. She said, 'I can't stand it anymore, and grabbed us by the ears and took us to a [Latin star] Celia Cruz concert. It really affected me." After that, Ricky broadened his musical interests to include other traditional Latin artists, like Tito Puente.

I Can Do That!

That Ricky could carry a tune and had a sweet voice was apparent early on, but so was his drive and ambition. From the time he started listening to music, he wanted to perform it. And from the time he started watching TV, he wanted to be *on* TV. As he related to *Interview* magazine, "At the age of six, I said, 'Dad, I want to be an artist.' My dad's a psychologist, my mother's an accountant, nobody in my family is in show business."

Not a problem. In that same interview, Ricky remembered his father's response: "'What did you say, "Kiki"? Because he calls me Kiki. How can I help you?' He was not," Ricky acknowledged, "a typical father."

In an MTV interview, Ricky related his father's words of wisdom. "You know what you want. You know what comes with all this. And you want to be in the spotlight. But you have to deal with the press. You

Ricky replaced the last original member of Menudo — in July 1984.

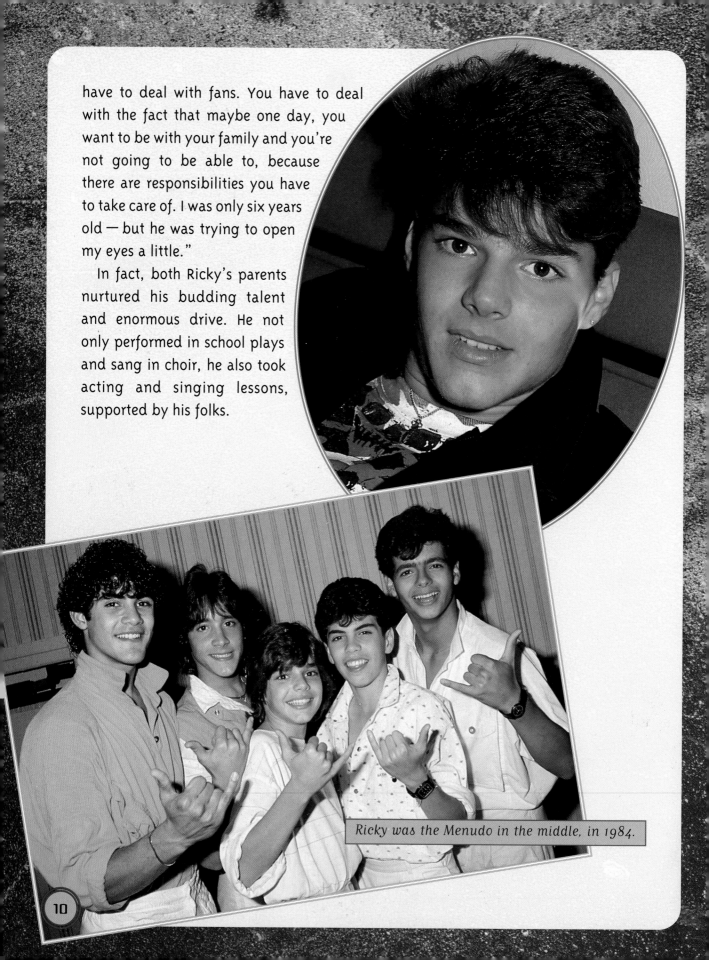

have to deal with fans. You have to deal with the fact that maybe one day, you want to be with your family and you're not going to be able to, because there are responsibilities you have to take care of. I was only six years old — but he was trying to open my eyes a little."

In fact, both Ricky's parents nurtured his budding talent and enormous drive. He not only performed in school plays and sang in choir, he also took acting and singing lessons, supported by his folks.

Ricky was the Menudo in the middle, in 1984.

He got his first shot at show biz at the age of six. Little Ricky tried out for a TV commercial, and snared it. "It was a soda commercial," he told *TV Week* magazine. "And after that, I did some [community] theater."

Ricky was certainly on his way to climbing the show biz ladder, but this was a little boy with outsize dreams — and his eye on a very specific and immediate prize.

Ricky and Robi Rosa remained close even after Menudo — today Robi is one of Ricky's producers.

See how he grew—in 1989, he was the tallest of the bunch (far left).

Boyz-2-Men-udo

That Ricky Martin spent five years in the most famous and successful boy group ever to come out of Puerto Rico, Menudo, is well chronicled. What's not so well-known is that it took Ricky three tries to get in the group.

He'd heard of the band, of course. He'd been a fan since its inception, in 1977: Ricky would've been little more than five! Even at that age, this is what he, as well as the rest of the pop-music world knew:

Menudo was a group of five boys, formed by music manager Edgardo Diaz. The boys wore matching outfits on stage, and sang pop ditties, thrilling adolescent audiences around the globe. Membership in Menudo fluctuated; the ages of the boys in the band is what stayed the same. Each had to be between 12–17 years old — upon reaching his 17th birthday, a boy was automatically "retired," making way for a new singer to join up.

Menudo takes over Disney World!

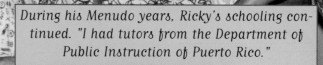

During his Menudo years, Ricky's schooling continued. "I had tutors from the Department of Public Instruction of Puerto Rico."

When Ricky Martin was 11, he wanted to be that new singer. In his official bio, he amends, "I didn't want to be a singer. What I wanted was to be in Menudo. I wanted to give concerts, to travel, to meet the pretty girls. I was always stubbornly determined to be one of them."

PERSISTENCE PAYS OFF

Ricky's dad helped him get his first audition. Correction: told him about a tryout, but didn't go with him. On-line, Ricky wrote, "My first audition, I took my bike and I showed up. I came back home, telling my parents that I was leaving to be an entertainer. I was eleven. They started laughing — then they started crying."

Well, not so fast. Ricky didn't snare the gig, not then, and not the second time he tried out, either. "The first two times I auditioned," he wrote in his record company bio, "they told me no, that I was too little." Ricky refused to give up hope. He knew that original group member, Ricky Melendez, was leaving and kept hoping to be the one to replace him. "They searched for his replacement for two years," says Ricky in his bio, "until they finally gave me a third audition and I turned out to be the one they chose."

ANSWER: *If you don't succeed the first time, try again.*
QUESTION: *Name a maxim that both Britney Spears and Ricky Martin believe in. She was rejected by* **The Mickey Mouse Club** *for being too small; he was rejected by* **Menudo** *for the same reason. Both eventually got those gigs — which turned out to be their big breaks.*

Even as far back as his Menudo days, Ricky felt music was a special way to communicate. "I believe the feelings and emotions I express in my music are universal," he says.

The date was July 10, 1984. Ricky would stick with Menudo for exactly five years; his date of departure was July 10, 1989.

Those five years were experience-soaked, "the best school," he declared. They also were filled with exhilarating ups and devastating downs. "I left my house when I was twelve years old, so I could have been a crazy little kid," he remarked in *Interview* magazine. A crazy little kid who might have grown up to be an unhappy adult.

That Ricky emerged fairly unscathed — that he chooses to see his experiences with the band as over-whelmingly positive — says more about who *he* is, than what *Menudo* was really like. Ricky Martin sees the bright side of all situations, finds the silver lining in what others see as clouds. Which is why he can say, today, of Menudo: "For me, it's been easy to forgive."

He's not, of course, in a state of denial. He knows he lost a lot of his childhood to long hours in recording studios — 16-hour sessions and rehearsals were not unheard of — airplanes, hotel rooms, and stages all over the world, as the group toured incessantly. "From the ages of twelve to seventeen, the most important

Just like a teenager — Ricky relaxes in his room, playing his guitar. (Wanna bet he was strumming one of his old Journey faves?!!!)

years of anyone's life, I had to ask permission to talk, and to move, and to go places," he said in an on-line interview. In *People* magazine he elaborated, "You weren't allowed to talk or express yourself. For five years, I couldn't go where I wanted, say what I wanted. Our creativity was stifled. We were told the songs we wrote were no good. We began to question the need for rehearsing the same routines over and over."

And then there is the flipside. Menudo made Ricky Martin a name, and also made him a millionaire. The band taught him

Ricky with his General Hospital co-star Lily Melgar. Though they were an on-screen romance, Lily admits they dated a couple of times, but remained "just friends."

discipline—how to be centered and focused as no other apprenticeship could have. It also taught him to appreciate his audience, no matter how big or how small. To fellow Latin music phenom Gloria Estefan, in *Interview* magazine, he described, "In Menudo I'd see two hundred and fifty thousand people from the stage in Brazil, and days later, there would be [only] fifteen people watching us. And the manager would say, 'You're going to perform like it's 250,000 people.' That's why [now] in each interview I do, each television show I appear on, it's going to be like the first one or the last one. That band definitely helped me keep my feet on the ground."

Ricky's positive feelings are echoed by another ex-Menudo member — perhaps the only one who has remained a close friend. Robi Rosa not only performed alongside Ricky in those days, today he is one of the main producers of Ricky's albums and co-wrote "Livin' *La Vida Loca*." In *Time* magazine, Robi explained, "Two things can happen when you join a group like Menudo. You get all messed up, or you can pay attention and learn from it. We learned a lot. For Ricky and me, the [recording] studio is like a home now."

The success Ricky enjoyed in Menudo was mind-blowing. During his years, the group released 16 albums, and had several number one singles. In the end, Ricky told *Smash Hits* magazine, "It was a phenomenal experience. Unfortunately, the rule was, you had to leave at seventeen. I am a man who cries, and I cried a lot."

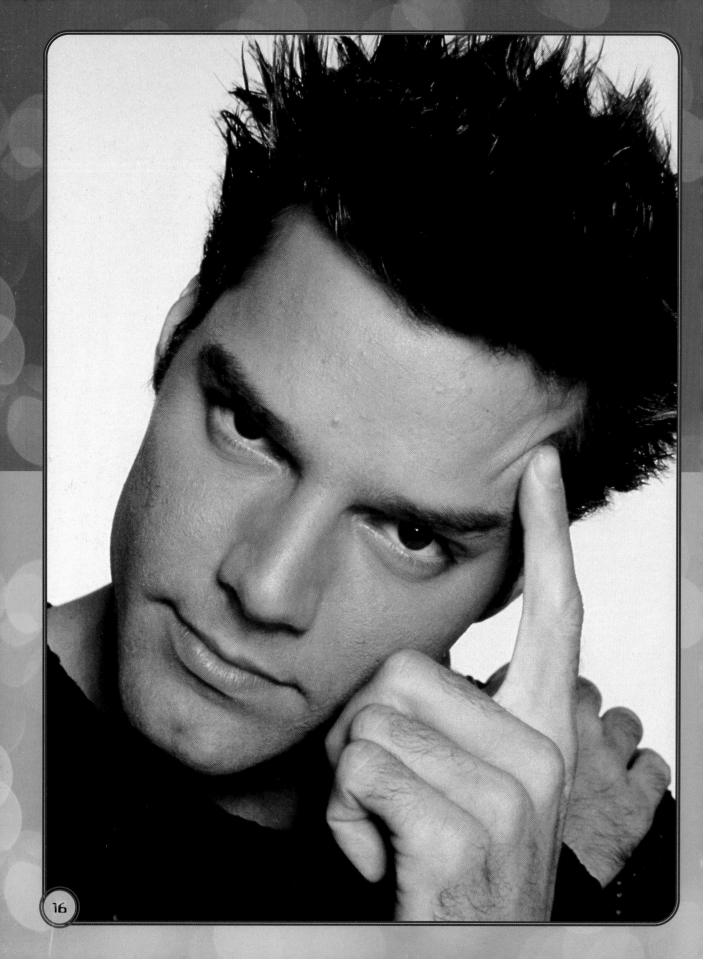

On His Own

When the Menudo bubble burst, Ricky made a major decision. After five years of constantly touring, running for safety from thousands of screaming girls, and being in the spotlight, Ricky wanted to be just Enrique again. So the conquering hero returned home to Puerto Rico and did something normal. He finished high school and hung out with his friends and family. In an interview with an on-line Latin music reporter, Ricky explained, "When I left the group, I took a whole year off just to spend some time with myself."

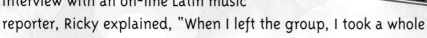

The Spotlight Beckons

During that year, Ricky did a lot of soul-searching. Here's what he found. He missed the joy of performing. By the end of 1989 he decided it was time to make yet another move.

"I was seventeen years old and I'd just moved to New York," Ricky told *Cleo* magazine. "I [had] told my mother I was going to New York for a vacation. Then, when I landed at the airport, I called her and told her I was staying. She went crazy. I started looking for an apartment, furniture, and things. But it was when I opened an [bank] account and signed the first check for the rent. I thought, 'Okay, this is it. I'm on my own now.' It felt amazing."

Ricky spent his time in New York making a plan. He went to the theater, he walked in the park, he consulted with acting and vocal teachers.

Ricky has always been an animal lover, but when he was in Menudo, he traveled so much, he had to leave his dog back home in Puerto Rico.

In a matter of months, Ricky took the next step in his career. He moved to Mexico to try the acting/singing waters there.

THE NEW RICKY

In Mexico, Ricky was basically on his own. He had no family there, but he was really getting into making his own professional decisions. He *had* made a lot of friends there during his Menudo years, so he adjusted to his surroundings fairly quickly.

However, it wasn't as easy as you might think — actually, there *was* something of a language barrier. Ricky recalls his first weeks there, trying to figure out the local lingo. "It was so different just being in another country where Spanish is spoken, but is almost another language," he said in an AOL on-line chat.

In the same on-line interview, Ricky also remembered being introduced to many encouraging and generous people in Mexico. "I was kind of adopted by this incredible family," he said. "They made it so much easier."

Helping the transition was an acting job. He quickly landed the role of "Pablo," the heartthrob of the Mexican soap opera, *Alcanzar Una Estrella II* (*To Reach a Star II*). The soap opera was so popular and Ricky so much in demand, that it was actually spun off into a feature film of the same name. That's when Ricky began collecting acting awards to go

Ricky and General Hospital co-star Lily Melgar made the daytime soap opera party scene.

along with his Menudo platinum records — he won the Heraldo (the Mexican Oscar) for the film *Más que Alcanzar Una Estrella*.

Though Ricky had put his music career on the back burner at this time, he never regretted it. "As a performer," he told a reporter, "I want to reach as many people as possible." *Alcanzar Una Estrella* did just that — and paved the way for Ricky's return to music. This time, he'd go solo.

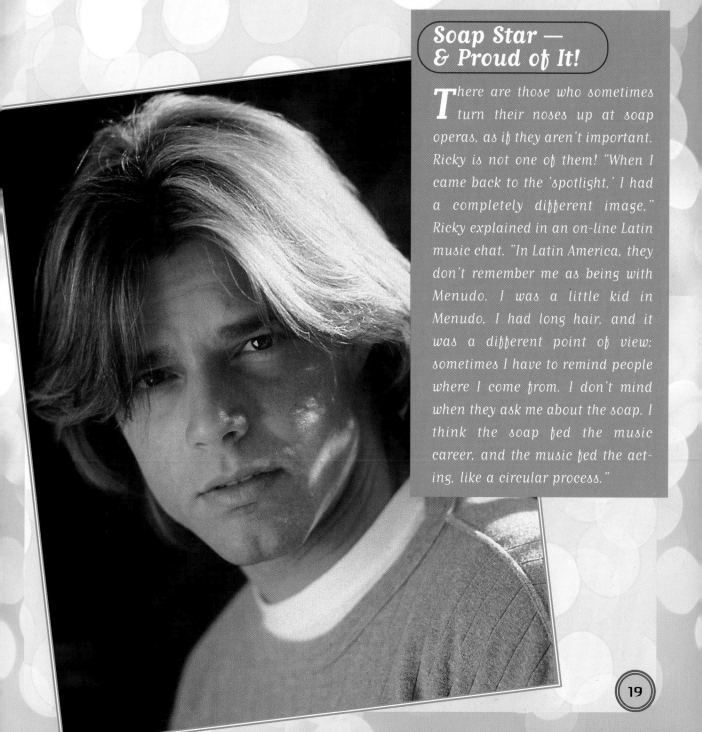

Soap Star — & Proud of It!

*T*here are those who sometimes turn their noses up at soap operas, as if they aren't important. Ricky is not one of them! "When I came back to the 'spotlight,' I had a completely different image," Ricky explained in an on-line Latin music chat. "In Latin America, they don't remember me as being with Menudo. I was a little kid in Menudo, I had long hair, and it was a different point of view; sometimes I have to remind people where I come from. I don't mind when they ask me about the soap. I think the soap fed the music career, and the music fed the acting, like a circular process."

"Once you do theater, it becomes kind of addictive and you have to do it again. It is one of the most beautiful things I've done in my life."

Ricky: The Heartthrob

GENERAL HOSPITAL HUNK

In 1994, Ricky was ready for another change. He wanted to return to the USA, and when he was offered a role on the popular ABC-TV soap opera *General Hospital* he jumped at it! Ricky was cast as "Miguel," a young man with a mysterious past. Miguel had been a pop star back in his home, Puerto Rico — talk about typecasting! — but he had left his beautiful island paradise to mend a broken heart. He settled in the town of Port Charles, where *General Hospital* takes place, and took a job as a bartender.

Naturally, half of the women in Port Charles fell for Miguel — and then the other half joined them when he returned to his first love: singing. This storyline gave the *GH* producers an opportunity to showcase Ricky's major appeal, and it also introduced a whole new American audience to Ricky Martin, the singer.

Ricky told *Rolling Stone* magazine that he considers *General Hospital* a major step forward. "It was great, but a bit crazy," he admitted. "[But] it helped me get in touch with myself, connect my heart and mind, and at the end of the day, it helped me a lot with my music."

Ricky, circa 1995. He and his golden retriever Icaro were inseparable.

Ricky has always loved music — from classic rock to salsa. His CD collection continues to grow!

ON STAGE IN LES MISÉRABLES

Indeed, *General Hospital* attracted some serious entertainment industry people to Ricky; though Ricky had never really been out of the recording studio — from 1991 to 1996 as a solo artist, Ricky had released three platinum-plus albums. *Ricky Martin*, *Me Amarás*, and *A Medio Vivir* were all huge hits throughout the Spanish-speaking world, as well as in Hispanic enclaves in the United States. But it was *General Hospital* that made the producers of Broadway's brilliant and long-running musical, *Les Misérables*, consider Ricky for the role of "Marius."

Ricky was quite nervous when he agreed to join the Broadway show. "In theater, if you miss [a line] . . . you miss!" he told a fan during an AOL on-line chat. "On TV you can cut and start the scene again. [In theater] it's always different, every night."

Ever the professional, Ricky fit right in with the *Les Miz* cast. "I never felt alone working with the actors that had been doing this show for many years," he continued during the chat. "The directors did an outstanding job. But at the same time I was so hungry for that role."

The months Ricky spent with *Les Miz* only helped prepare him for his next adventure. "Theater is great," he said in a recent MTV interview. "That's exactly when you have to

Music industry big time — Sony Records' top guy, Tommy Mottola; Celine Dion; and Ricky.

really understand the meaning of the word discipline. It's seven shows a week, and it's three hours on stage and running. You're dealing with classical sounds. You're dealing with a different audience every night. If you want a standing ovation, you have to sweat. I have a lot of respect for theater actors — if you can do that, you can do anything you want in life. And I loved it!"

"I want you!" Ricky sings.

Just Wondering

One of your most popular songs is "María" — is there a real María?

"She was a very intense computer program! I wanted to get closer to my roots, to my culture. We started digging around, looking for sounds and rhythms on the computer and that's how it came about — it wasn't any specific girl. I mean, María could be anyone. I can be very romantic — stupidly romantic, but not in this case." (Cleo mag)

Has a girl ever inspired a song of yours?

"Not just songs, but whole albums. Unfortunately, it's usually after you break up with someone and the pain is still raw that you find the need to express it in a very dramatic way. That's when it becomes music." (Cleo)

What do you want your audience to feel when they hear your music?

"I want them to feel free, liberated. I want them to be who they are with my music. . . . Being on stage — that adrenaline, it's amazing. Imagine all your senses are on. You're seeing people going crazy, dancing, and having fun with your music. That's your mission: to make them go crazy." (Interview)

Ricky Martin

Ricky Martin Facts at Your Fingertips

Ricky holds his multi-platinum CD, Vuelve.

BASIC STATS

Given Name: Enrique José Martin Morales
Nickname: Kiki
Stage Name: Ricky Martin
Birthday: December 24, 1971
Birthplace: Santurce, Puerto Rico
Sun Sign: Capricorn
Current Residence: Miami, Florida
Previous Residences: Brazil, Mexico, Argentina
Hair/Eyes: Black-dark brown/black-dark brown
Height/Weight: 6'2"/165 lbs
Parents: Nereida Morales and Enrique Martin Negroni — they divorced when Ricky was two years old
Brothers: Fernando, Daniel, and Eric
Sister: Vanessa
Tattoo: A flower and a heart (he won't reveal where but says getting the tattoo was "very painful!")

FAVORITES

Color: Black
Cities: San Juan, Puerto Rico and Miami, Florida
Vacation: Rio de Janeiro
Beach: Palominito — it's on the northeast side of Puerto Rico
Childhood Musical Artists: Journey, Annie Lennox, Boston
Current Musical Artists: Maxwell, Miguel Bose, Sting

Music: All kinds — especially rock and salsa

Type of Foods: Italian, Chinese

Fast Food: Hamburgers, pizza

Movie: *In the Name of the Father*

Fashion Designer: Georgio Armani — Ricky has even modeled at Armani fashion shows

Books: *La Tregua* by Mario Benedetti

Poets: Ángel Morales (Ricky's grandfather), T.S. Eliot, Arthur Rimbaud, Federico García Lorca, Mario Benedetti

Actor: Robert De Niro

TV Talk Show Host: Rosie O'Donnell

Relaxation: A bubble bath

Pastime: Reading and writing poetry

Place to Just Think: A park

RICKY THE ACTOR

Theater

• The Mexican musical *Mamá Ama el Rock* (*Mama Loves Rock*)

• The Broadway musical *Les Misérables* (Marius)

Television

• He played "Pablo" on the most popular Mexican daytime soap opera *Alcanzar Una Estrella II* (*To Reach a Star II*)

What was it like to sing a duet with Madonna? "We're talking about a legend here," Ricky told Rolling Stone. "She's amazing."

• The short-lived NBC-TV sitcom, *Getting By*

• He played "Miguel Morez" on the top-rated ABC-TV soap opera *General Hospital* (1994–1996)

The Big Screen

• The movie version of *Más que Alcanzar Una Estrella* (1990)

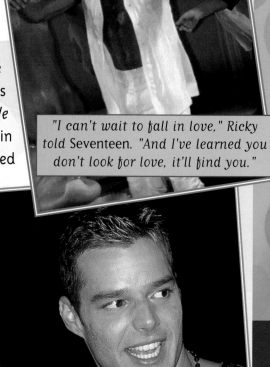

1 In the Spanish version of the Disney animated film *Hercules*, Ricky was the voice of the he-man himself!

2 Ricky owns the restaurant, Casa Salsa, in the trendy South Beach section of Miami. It features gourmet Puerto Rican cuisine. In a recent *People* magazine, a recipe for Grilled Fillet of Tuna in Rum-Molasses Sauce from Casa Salsa was featured — but Ricky's *least* favorite food is seafood! (Ricky loves to cook — his specialty is Italian food.)

"I can't wait to fall in love," Ricky told Seventeen. "And I've learned you don't look for love, it'll find you."

3 Ricky started his professional career doing commercials in Puerto Rico. His two biggest ones were for Pepsi Cola and Kellogg's cereals.

4 Did you know that the handsome young man who invites you to come visit Puerto Rico in those national TV commercials is none other than Ricky Martin?

5 In Puerto Rico it's against the law to serenade someone outside their house because of the noise. But when Ricky lived in Mexico he recalls: "Sometimes I would go to a plaza full of mariachi bands and we would get a bunch of us together and go to a friend's house to dance, sing, and play," Ricky told *Cleo* magazine. "It wasn't actually a serenade, but it could get romantic."

6 Julio Iglesias is Ricky's major musical influence. Ricky refers to the Latin crooner as his "godfather." "I have been able to work with him and he's given me wise [advice]," Ricky revealed on-line. "I really do admire him. I don't want to be him, but I want to follow in his footsteps."

Conduc
agiera - José Mol
Music Produc
ze - Phil Ramo
ite abitua
anopavarotti
to del Carlino
NAZIONE
GIORNO
RADIO
167-75264

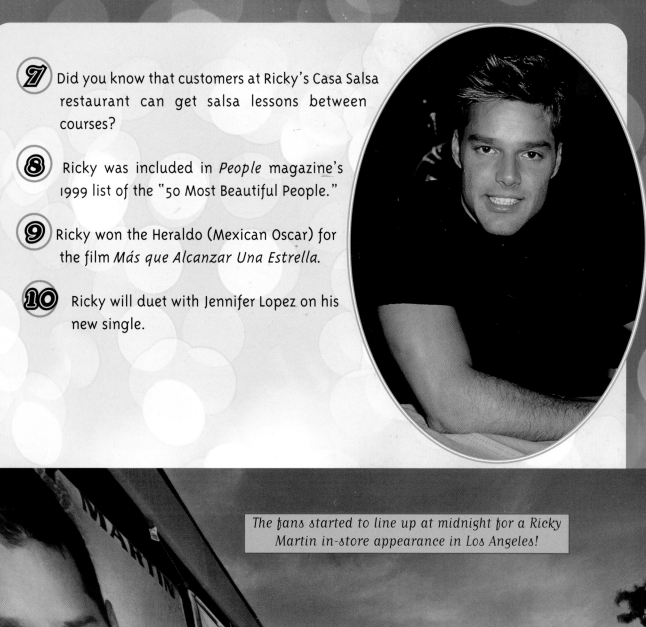

7 Did you know that customers at Ricky's Casa Salsa restaurant can get salsa lessons between courses?

8 Ricky was included in *People* magazine's 1999 list of the "50 Most Beautiful People."

9 Ricky won the Heraldo (Mexican Oscar) for the film *Más que Alcanzar Una Estrella*.

10 Ricky will duet with Jennifer Lopez on his new single.

The fans started to line up at midnight for a Ricky Martin in-store appearance in Los Angeles!

Around the World With Ricky

When the chimes rang at midnight to call in the new year of 1998, Ricky Martin had no idea it was going to be the year that turned his life around!

In 1998, Ricky released his fourth solo album, *Vuelve*. By the time it hit the stores, it was already a major hit. Combined, his four solo albums had sold more than fifteen million copies and he had number one hit songs in dozens of countries.

¡Viva La Ricky!

It was a performance in France that really made 1998 the year to remember for Ricky. He performed the soccer anthem *"La Copa de la Vida"* at the 1998 World Cup championship. The soccer fans went ballistic. They cheered for Ricky almost as much as they did for the competing teams.

Ricky was thrilled. Not only had the crowd in the stadium responded so well, but he realized the World Cup was beamed by satellite all over the world. "At least one billion [saw me]!" he exclaimed on an Australian radio show, *Hey, Hey, It's Saturday*. "It was a fascinating experience, but I was ready for it because I had been working on this project for more than a month and I was just dying to be there. It was a fascinating way to exchange cultures. There were more than a billion people watching me perform my music. My music is my rhythms, my sound, and it's the way I present where I come from. It was fascinating. The audience

Proud Ricky shows off the award he received in Madrid, Spain, for selling 600,000 copies of Vuelve.

was very warm. The reactions and comments from the international media was also very positive."

POSITIVITY

The reaction was so positive that the bigwigs at Ricky's music label, Sony International, decided it was time to let the English-speaking part of the world get a taste of his talent, too. The executives moved him over to their brand-new label, C2 — established for "sure hits" — and had Ricky record *Ricky Martin*. The American audience had their appetites whetted when he performed "*La Copa de la Vida*" at the Grammys, but when the album hit the stores in early May 1999, well, let's just say the rest is history. In a matter of weeks the album and the single were resting high on top of the Latin and pop charts . . . and Ricky was getting to really live the crazy life!

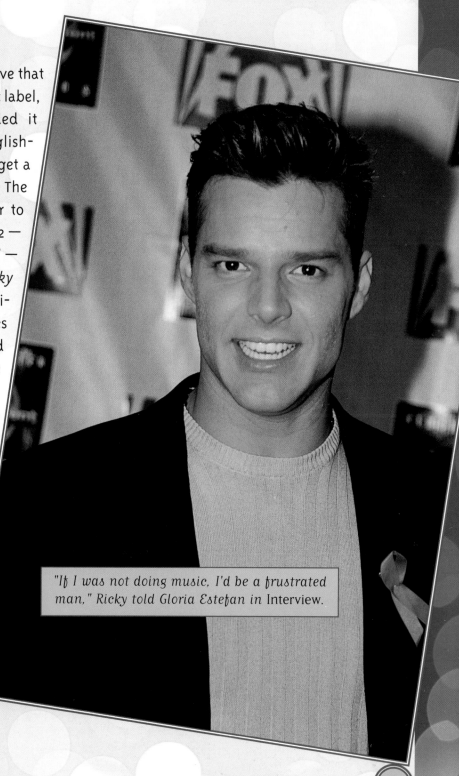

"If I was not doing music, I'd be a frustrated man," Ricky told Gloria Estefan in Interview.

Loca-Motion!

"I'm Flying! I'm Flying!"

That's Ricky's reaction to his red-hot success. And check it: He's not likely to land on terra firma any time soon. The May 1999 release of his debut album in English, *Ricky Martin,* took care of that — it zoomed to number one right out of the box, selling an astounding 661,000 copies its first week. It ranks among the top twenty debuts of all time. What's so amazing about it? *Ricky Martin,* the album, fuses English and Spanish words with Latin rhythms to create a fresh new energy. Some call it Latin pop, other say it's a mixture of salsa, rumba, mambo, hip-hop, and dance-pop. There are 14 tracks altogether . . . of course, American audiences already had a taste of at least one of them. That one made all the difference.

Ricky rocked New York during his free, live concert for The Today Show. *"Livin' La Vida Loca," was the fan favorite.*

Livin' La Vida Loca

"We wanted to write *the* millennium party song," said composer/producer Desmond Child and the riotously infectious "Livin' *La Vida Loca*" is what came out. It's the frantically paced, dance-ready song that propelled Ricky to the very "crazy life" of the lyrics, to tippy-top of the fame-and-fortune-o-meter. This one may always be Ricky's signature song, but a few others on the album are just as pungent.

Be Careful (Cuidado Con Mi Corazón)

The duet with Madonna was planned as a surprise: the Latin boy sings in English; the American girl, in Spanish. Ricky and Madonna had met several times before the Grammys; they'd never

Even teen queen Love Hewitt wants to get next to Ricky!

really connected before, however. In *USA Today*, Ricky related the story of how he felt when Madonna suggested a duet. "Madonna's into a changing culture, she always has been. She enjoys the Latin sounds. She's energetic, I'm energetic." Neither superstar was even sure whose album the song would fit on, but that didn't seem important.

"Let's just have fun," Ricky recalled telling her.

The Best of the Rest

Those songs may be the most well-known on the album, but others are vibin' just the same. Want slow romantic tunes? Check out, "She's All I Ever Had" and "I Am Made of You." Looking to dance and sing along with Rico-suave? Get down with "Shake Your Bon-Bon" and "Love You for a Day." And then there's "María," a song that's already a hit all over the world — the version on this album is "Spanglish." His anthem, *"La Copa de la Vida,"* is, of course, on the album as well.

Latin pop is poised to be the next hot thing in music — and no one ignites the genre better than Ricky Martin. Ricky writes lyrics — only not in English, not yet. He feels he needs a little more work on the language before he could compose in it.

Ricky amazed the crowd at El Monte, California, when he performed on the Spanish holiday, Cinco de Mayo.

Why English? Why Now?

*T*hat's a question tossed at Ricky nearly everywhere he goes. His enormous success with Spanish and European fans already made him a superstar — why the need to "crossover" as it's called in the music biz? And why now?

The *short* answer is that Ricky was finally ready. In Time magazine he said, "Everything I do, I do when I'm ready. So now is the moment."

The *real* answer, is that it was always part of the grand plan. This was a talent who'd already made it — as an actor, certainly, and with Menudo — in the USA. So why wouldn't he want to release an album that his American fans could understand and relate to? It made perfect sense: it was just a matter of time.

As he told People on-line, "It's all about communication." He'd already communicated musically with the rest of the world, and as he said in New York's Daily News, "Recording in English was just the next logical step."

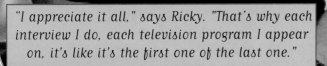

"I appreciate it all," says Ricky. "That's why each interview I do, each television program I appear on, it's like it's the first one of the last one."

Ricky: On Stage Sigh Guy

The experience of Ricky live is awesome — he's on tour now!

"Being on stage. That adrenaline, it's amazing," says Ricky of performing for an audience. "Imagine all your senses are on."

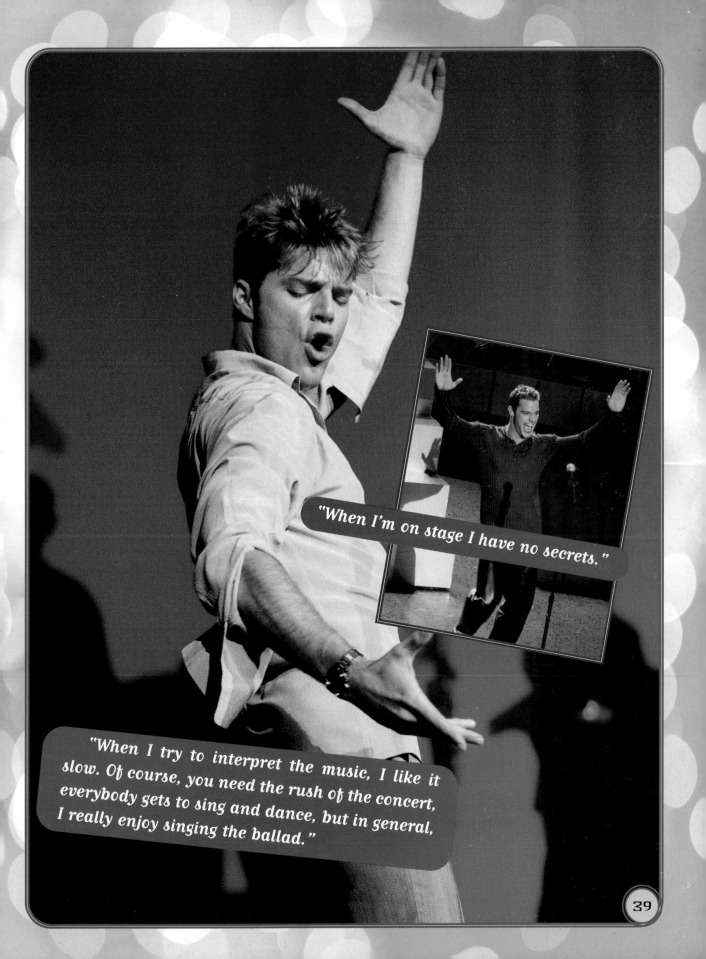

"When I'm on stage I have no secrets."

"When I try to interpret the music, I like it slow. Of course, you need the rush of the concert, everybody gets to sing and dance, but in general, I really enjoy singing the ballad."

Ricky amazed the crowd at El Monte, California, when he performed on the Spanish holiday, Cinco de Mayo.

From the stage, Ricky loves to see people enjoying the music. "You see people going crazy, dancing, and having fun with your music. That's your mission: to make them go crazy."

"It's a challenge you have every time you go on stage: to make people change their minds about what a culture could be. The first thing I might say is, 'We're here to forget about who we are. Let's be free. Let's forget about problems in life and work and home.'"

The Real Ricky: Up Close and Personal

"In this business, you have to be in touch with yourself, because you can go crazy if you're not." That was a lesson, Ricky remarked in *Interview* magazine, that he learned in Menudo. It's one he's carried with him always.

Ricky's fans range in age from 8 to 80!

Music, acting, performing, entertaining — livin' *la vida loca* — may be Ricky's life. His heart, and his soul, however, have other claims on them. First and foremost: his family and his heritage, followed closely by his friends, fans, his spiritual life, and his romantic life.

FAMILY TIES

Ricky's extended family includes not only his parents, but step-siblings from both sides. They include the older brothers, Fernando and Daniel he grew up with, and two sibs from his dad's second marriage, Eric and Vanessa. He sees all of them as often as he can.

"Family is so important to me," he wrote in an official bio. "When I feel lonely on the road, I just take a deep breath and think about them — where I've come from, where I'm going, and where I am. My mom is my best friend. I can talk to her about my innermost feelings."

As he expressed in *Smash Hits* magazine, "I speak to my family a lot. My whole family is in Puerto Rico, but my family is my balance. My mother pulls my ears every time she sees I need it."

Ricky's family also helps run his company, Ikaro.

HOMELAND & HERITAGE: "I AM PUERTO RICO"

"My house is in Miami. Puerto Rico is my home." That distinction, which Ricky has made to many reporters, says it all. He has always been proud of his homeland and his heritage, but the real bonus of his white-hot fame is the chance Ricky now has to talk about it.

It's a chance for him to revel in the beauty of his homeland, and of its people. Ricky even stars in tourism ads for the common-wealth of Puerto Rico.

More important, maybe, is that Ricky can now be a stereotype-smasher. "I'm very proud of my culture," he said in an on-line interview, "and I understand that stereotypes come from ignorance. The best way to change people's minds is to teach people."

In *Entertainment Weekly* he elaborated, "For me, the fact that people think Puerto Rico is [the gang movie] *Scarface*, that we ride donkeys to school — that has to change." He refused to star in a remake of the famous musical *West Side Story*. "It's kicking my culture, and I'm not gonna feed that." He even attributes his Grammy performance success to a bit of stereotype-smashing. "They see a Latin guy," Ricky remarked about that American TV appearance, "they were expecting the ranchero hat on his head and then something modern came out, something refreshing, very energetic."

His fans totally get it. "He's given Puerto Ricans so much to be proud of," one fan who was quoted in a New York newspaper said. "He represents us."

Gettin' Spicy Wit' It!

*T*ourist tip: Check out the restaurant at 524 Ocean Drive in Miami Beach, Florida. Called Casa Salsa, it's owned by Ricky Martin and features Puerto Rican cuisine at its most savory. Any chance of a Ricky-sighting at the next table? If he's in town . . .absolutely!

THE FRIENDSHIP EXPRESS

The tough thing about making new friends when you're famous is never knowing why friendships are offered: Is it because you're a star, or because of who you are? Ricky's reaction to that dilemma is to keep close ties with the people who knew him before he reached mega-stardom. "My friends are the ones I had in school," he told *Smash Hits* magazine. He added in an on-line interview, "If I had one wish, it would be to bring all my friends with me, every time I go on the road. And some day, I'll do that."

THE CORAZÓN QUESTION

"I'm very romantic. I like spilling my guts," Ricky said in *YM* magazine. No question he brings real emotion to his romantic ballads. But he doesn't often get to practice the lyrics he pours his heart into. Isn't it ironic: livin' *la vida loca* allows him little time for a love life. "Music is very jealous," he says. "Years ago, I would have given up everything and would have done anything for love — but not now. Maybe that's because I haven't met the right woman," he once said in the Australian magazine *Cleo*. Would he know such a soulmate if he found her? Perhaps. He certainly knows the qualities he's looking for, as he listed in *TeenBeat* magazine.

"I look for faithfulness and intelligence. I love a woman with high self-esteem. She has to know what she wants, and be determined and independent."

Ask Ricky to get specific though, and mostly, he gets elusive. He's talked about an on-again, off-again girlfriend named Rebecca de Alba, who lives and works in Spain as a TV presenter. They met when he was 18 and according to published reports, have been seeing each other ever since.

However, he recently told *Access Hollywood*, "We broke up."

Ricky admits being into fashion; even if he weren't in show biz, he'd be into the trends. He's worked with Georgio Armani.

FAN-DE-MONIUM

Ricky has über-respect and love for his fans — and in his experience, those fans feel the same way toward him. In *TeenBeat,* he allowed, "Fans are the bosses. It's important to have communication with them. I don't duck them. I want a little privacy and they know that. I'm human and so are they."

In *Tell* magazine he continued, "Sometimes fans do get out of control, but they just want to let you know what they feel. They knock on the door — hello, I'm here! I want to talk to you. Or, maybe they say 'I love you.'"

Communicating with his fans through his music is what Ricky's all about. In an official bio written when Ricky was 21, he expressed his fan-feelings. "I feel as if I have to put out what I think, so my fans know how I feel . . . I want them to grow along with me. The most important thing is to be honest with them about what I've done to get where I am. In my life, I've done a great deal and I can share my experiences with them."

WHERE THE SPIRIT MOVES HIM

"I need to be alone [to recharge]. I need to spend some time with myself. I need to connect heart and mind . . . so next time I walk on stage, I can be honest. It's necessary. It's healthy."

Ricky meditates every morning and practices yoga. "The goal is to find serenity," and yoga helps him stay grounded and focused. As he expressed in *USA Today*, "In this business, you deal with so much fantasy . . . the adrenaline is constantly going. I've got to have twenty to forty minutes a day to myself and ask myself how I'm affecting others, how I'm letting others affect me, and not be harmed."

It was on a trip to India that Ricky had what he terms a spiritual awakening. He explained in *Newsweek*, "I felt a comfort I never felt before. I you listen to Hindu music, it connects to the Gypsy music from Spain, which connects back to Latin America."

Now, after every concert, Ricky closes with a reverent bow, which in India is called a *namaste*.

HOME SWEET HOME

Along with Sting, Ricky performed in a concert to benefit the Rainforest Foundation.

At home in Miami, Ricky goes into high-speed relax mode. He lives in pajamas, which are pants and sweats to him, cooks *in*, as opposed to eating *out*, and chills by taking bubble baths, or going to the beach and just looking at the ocean. Ricky rarely checks the mirror, and almost never checks out the party scene — which in Miami's South Beach is major. Ricky's attitude about that is a total "been there, done that, don't want to do it anymore." Keeping in drool-worthy shape is something he works at — daily visits to the gym, rock-climbing and mountain biking are his exercises of choice.

"My priority at this moment is for Latin music to be respected."

He's soft-spoken and polite and without disrespecting his fans, tries to keep his private life out of the public spotlight. "When I'm on stage, I have no secrets," he told *USA Today*. "But I try to protect the privacy of my room, my house, my friends, my family. In Miami, my backyard is a bay and when I walk out the back door of the house, I have to make sure there's nobody on a boat taking pictures."

LIFE ACCORDING TO RICKY

He admits to a bit of moodiness as well. In an MTV interview, he revealed, "I have my ups and downs. I'm human. I breathe to have a heart that beats, and sometimes I just don't want to leave my house. I want to stay at home and relax — and sometimes I want to quit, because you have to deal with a lot of sacrifices. Sometimes I feel weak. Sometimes I'm afraid. So it's important to take my time and . . . analyze what I've done. Step out of the picture . . . look at the picture, look at what you've done, where you are, where you want to get, and go back . . . with a healthier way of thinking."

Discography-Plus

SPANISH-LANGUAGE ALBUMS

Ricky Martin (1991)
Hit Singles
- "Fuego Contra Fuego"
- "Dime Que Me Quieres"

Me Amarás (1993)
Hit Singles
- "Me Amarás"
- "Lo Que Nos Pase Pasará"

A Medio Vivir (1996)
Hit Singles
- "María"
- "Nada es Imposible"
- "Fuego de Noche"
- "Nieve de Día"

Vuelve (1998)
Hit Singles
- "Vuelve"

"I won! I won! — Ricky at the 1999 Grammys.

DEBUT ENGLISH-LANGUAGE ALBUM

Ricky Martin (1999)

- **First Single:** "Livin' *La Vida Loca*" — soared to the number one spot on both the Spanish and pop charts within weeks of release.

Single Tracks
1. "Livin' *La Vida Loca*" (English)
2. "Spanish Eyes"
3. "She's All I Ever Had"
4. "Shake Your Bon-Bon"
5. "Be Careful *Cuidado Con Mi Corazón*" (with Madonna)

6. "I Am Made of You"
7. "Love You for a Day"
8. "Private Emotion" (with Meja)
9. "The Cup of Life" (Spanglish)
10. "You Stay With Me"
11. "Livin' *La Vida Loca*" (Spanish)
12. "I Count the Minutes"
13. "Bella"
14. "María" (Spanglish)

"I've had my ups and downs. And I'm very proud of them. Every step of the way."

Get in Touch With Ricky:

Latin Music On-Line:
www.lamusica.com/ricky.htm

Fan Club: Ricky Martin Fan Club
P.O. Box 13345
Santurce Station
San Juan, Puerto Rico
00908-3345

Menudo Albums With Ricky Martin

* *Reaching Out (1984)*
* *Evolución (1984)*
* *Mania (1984*
* *16 Greatest Hits (1984)*
* *Menudo: 1985 (1985)*
* *Ayer y Hoy (1985)*
* *Refrescante (1986)*
* *Festa Vai Comecar (1986)*
* *Menudo: 1986 (1986)*
* *Can't Get Enough (1986)*
* *Viva Bravo (1986)*
* *Somos Los Hijos del Rock (1987)*
* *Menudo in Action (1988)*
* *The Best of Menudo (1988)*
* *Sons of Rock (1988)*
* *Sombras Y Figuras (1989)*

Looking Ahead

"I want to do this forever."
— Ricky in *Time* magazine

He's been performing pretty much all his life — and that's exactly what Ricky Martin intends to do with the rest of it. "Longevity is very important to me," he told New York's *Daily News.* "I don't want this to be just a passing thing. In ten to fifteen years, I still want to be doing music. That's what I'm working for."

But what frontiers are left to conquer for Ricky Martin, global-guy? I'd like to do it all," he answers. "People ask me what I'll be doing thirty years from now and I tell them I'll be in the entertainment business; singing, acting, maybe even producing. I was born for this. I enjoy what I do."

Ricky realizes, "Fame can be fatal. The day this isn't fun anymore, I quit. Before, I was working to forget problems in my life. Today, I'm working because I'm having a good time."

Although music will always come first, Ricky allows for other possibilities. If the right movie came along, he'd do it. If a fantastic stage role were offered, he'd take it. And if he got the chance to produce, direct, and spend six months out of the spotlight, writing — well, that looks pretty good to him, too.

Ricky's immediate plans, however, include lots of touring — a coast-to-coast US tour is what he's in the middle of right now. It will take him well into 2000. And when all is said and done, that's where his heart is. As Ricky quipped in *Interview* magazine, "If I weren't a musician, I would be the most frustrated man. I'd be working at Burger King, knocking down doors, begging, 'Can I sing? Let me sing!'"

To that, a grateful world responds, "You go!!"